THE ROOKERY

A BUILDING BOOK FROM
THE CHICAGO
ARCHITECTURE FOUNDATION

JAY PRIDMORE

PHOTOGRAPHS BY
HEDRICH BLESSING

Pomegranate

SAN FRANCISCO

Published by Pomegranate Communications, Inc.
Box 808022, Petaluma California 94975
800 227 1428; www.pomegranate.com

Pomegranate Europe Ltd.
Unit 1, Heathcote Business Centre, Hurlbutt Road
Warwick, Warwickshire CV34 6TD, U. K.
sales@pomeurope.co.uk

Library of Congress Cataloging-in-Publication Data
Pridmore, Jay.
    The Rookery : a building book from the Chicago Architecture Foundation/
    Jay Pridmore ; photographs by Hedrich Blessing.
        p. cm.
    ISBN 978-0-7649-2306-7 (alk. paper)
        1. Rookery Building (Chicago, Ill.) 2. Burnham and Root. 3. Chicago (Ill.)—Buildings,
structures, etc. I. Blessing, Hedrich. II. Chicago Architecture Foundation. III. Title.

NA6233.C4 R667 2003
725'.23—dc21

                                                        2002030789

Pomegranate Catalog No. A660
Cover and book design by Shannon Lemme
Printed in Korea
20 19 18 17 16 15 14 13 12 11   10 9 8 7 6 5 4 3 2

MISSION

The Chicago Architecture Foundation (CAF) is dedicated to advancing public interest and education in architecture and related design. CAF pursues this mission through a comprehensive program of tours, lectures, exhibitions, special programs, and youth programs, all designed to enhance the public's awareness and appreciation of Chicago's important architectural legacy.

Founded in 1966, the Chicago Architecture Foundation has evolved to become a nationally recognized resource advancing public interest and education in Chicago's outstanding architecture. Its programs serve more than 350,000 people each year. For more information contact us at the address below, or visit us on our website:

> Chicago Architecture Foundation
> 224 South Michigan Avenue
> Chicago IL 60604
> 312-922-TOUR (8687)
> www.architecture.org

ACKNOWLEDGMENTS

The Building Book series has benefited greatly from the collaboration of many people with an interest in Chicago's architecture and the mission of the Chicago Architecture Foundation. The Rookery, in particular, has had the wholehearted and indispensable support of several key groups and individuals.

At Hedrich Blessing, Mike Houlahan and Bob Shimer made this book possible by opening their archive and making new photographs. At McClier, T. Gunny Harboe, AIA, Vice President of the firm's Preservation Group, provided enormous input and was unstinting in his review of the manuscript and photographs as they were assembled; Doug Gilbert was most helpful in the search for photographs. At Vinci/Hamp Architects, Inc., John Vinci and Ward Miller were of great assistance in accessing the Richard Nickel Archive.

At the Rookery itself, we thank Jeannine Rio, assistant general manager for Clarion Realty Services. We are also grateful to publisher Katie Burke and managing editor Eva Strock of Pomegranate Communications for their enthusiasm and work in making this and other Building Books a reality.

We would also like to acknowledge the work of the CAF's in-house staff and freelancers, who conceived, assembled, and promoted the Building Book series, including Bonita Mall, vice president of programs; Ellen Christensen, architectural consultant; Jay Pridmore, author; and Ed Hirschland, editor, who also generously gave us access to his library.

Lynn J. Osmond, President and CEO

ROOKERY CHRONOLOGY

1871   The Great Chicago Fire destroys most of Chicago. Plans are quickly made to rebuild the city greater than ever.

1872   Architect John Wellborn Root, age 22, arrives in Chicago from New York.

1873   Root joins Daniel H. Burnham as partner, and the firm Burnham & Root begins to build nearly two dozen tall buildings in the Loop.

1885   The Home Insurance Building, reputed to be the world's first metal-framed skyscraper, is built by William Le Baron Jenney at LaSalle and Adams Streets, across the street from the site of the Rookery.

1887–1888   The Rookery is built on the site of the old City Hall, which had been called a "rookery" because of the crows living in its exterior walls and the crooked politicians inside. The new building features hybrid construction—masonry walls on the outside and a metal frame supporting the walls of the light court within.

1905–1907   The Rookery's first interior renovation is designed and executed by Frank Lloyd Wright, covering much of Root's wrought iron ornament with panels of incised Carrara marble.

1931   The second interior renovation of the Rookery is designed and executed by William Drummond. A modernized interior includes enclosed elevators, Art Deco detailing, and an iron staircase protruding into the light court.

1992   A third major renovation of the Rookery, by Baldwin Development Company and the architects of McClier, applies state-of-the-art restoration techniques to bring the Rookery back to its early splendor and to create first-class rental office space in the LaSalle Street financial district.

Among historic buildings of Chicago, the Rookery on LaSalle Street reigns as an undisputed favorite. Its vivid design attracts architects and historians. Its lofty atrium attracts tourists from around the world. Its red granite facade at the lower floors remains a symbol of old Chicago, and it has been studied and analyzed since the time it was built in 1888.

Yet the Rookery defies easy categorization. Its architect, John Wellborn Root, for example, was an early exponent of the Chicago School of commercial architecture, the movement that sought beauty in the plain and unadorned office building, but the Rookery is elaborate and highly decorative. It has been called modern for its use of large, light-filling windows, yet elements of its design reach back to antiquity.

What is not ambiguous is the power of the Rookery, not only as an example of original architecture, but also as a living and useful monument in Chicago's teeming commercial center. In a neighborhood of skyscrapers that are larger, more soaring in profile, and frankly more profitable as real estate, the Rookery has survived the trend to raze old buildings and erase memories of eras past. Its striking recent restoration has revived the Rookery as a first-class office building, and more than that, it heralds a resurgence in the delicate but timeless values of Root and his creative architectural mind.

Photograph by Nick Merrick of Hedrich Blessing, courtesy McClier

In 1888, when the Rookery was completed, architect John Wellborn Root achieved a building of "structural expression," as he termed his goal of showing and not hiding the way the pieces were assembled. He also created a building of striking beauty.

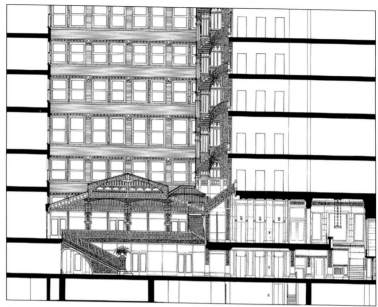

"It is not the style, but the plan of the building that makes it of great importance," wrote the architect and critic Thomas E. Tallmadge of the Rookery in 1927. As the section drawing shown here and the floor plan (opposite) illustrate, the Rookery maximizes rentable office space filled with abundant natural light.

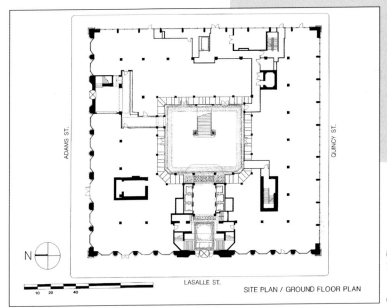

ADAMS ST.

QUINCY ST.

N

LASALLE ST.

SITE PLAN / GROUND FLOOR PLAN

10 20   40

Courtesy McClier

In the early 1900s, novelist Theodore Dreiser compared Chicago, where he set his gritty novels, to the Florence of Michelangelo and the Medici. This required imagination on Dreiser's part, since Chicago was overwhelmingly industrial, its air smoky, and its merchant princes, as often as not, corrupt beyond compare. But it was also a place of such contrasts, such intensity, and so downright American in its promise of wealth that artists flocked to Chicago to comprehend it all.

Chicago's role as a great commercial center was cast in 1836 when construction began on a canal that would connect the Great Lakes to the Mississippi River basin. It grew like a city of destiny from then on, becoming an international marvel after the Great Chicago Fire of 1871, followed by a rebuilding effort the likes of which no city had ever undertaken before.

Post-Fire Chicago inspired creativity in many branches of the arts. Among them, new literature grew from the living legends of commerce. The titans of the Stock Exchange and Board of Trade were transmuted into American fiction—in novels such as *Sister Carrie* by Dreiser and *The Pit* by Frank Norris. The higher spirits of inspiration touched Chicago architecture as well. Buildings of such size and force went up that they naturally attracted the brightest architectural lights of the age, those who would define the next phase of American architecture. It was the beginning of what we now know as modern architecture.

Today, the Rookery on LaSalle Street stands as a staunch symbol of this period and innovative spirit. Curiously, perhaps, it appears to be from

The Rookery had many modern elements, but the intricacy of its detail harked back to the days when buildings were a reflection of the many hands that worked on them.

Photograph Bill Engdahl © Hedrich Blessing

another age—a dark, quiet facade of stone, described as Moorish by early observers and antique today compared to its more recent neighbors.

Still, the Rookery introduced many breakthroughs at a time when architecture was on the verge of adopting new technologies: metal framing, fireproofing, elevators, and plate glass among them. In the Rookery, Root employed all these technologies—all closely tied to the development of skyscrapers—while meeting the entirely modern need for commodious and abundant rental space in the Loop.

Burnham and Root's library, where the partners (Burnham at left, Root at right) were photographed, show that the architects found suitable quarters in the Rookery, a building that they designed.

The 1992 restoration of the old library shows a labor of love for the architects of McClier and their clients at Baldwin Development. A new copy of the *Venus de Milo* was found for the mantel, and the rug was custom-loomed to match the original.

As one of Chicago's best-loved buildings, the Rookery has the light court as its centerpiece.
Root may have been glancing at the drawings of Piranesi when he designed the Rookery, or
perhaps he was thinking about the great open spaces of modern Parisian department stores.
But clearly he was also creating what Donald Hoffmann calls "a most fantastic aviary,"
inspired by the building's whimsical name.

The Rookery may appear to be from another age, but in one critical respect it is entirely of ours. Its design is a rich example of how form and function together were guiding the quest for a new type of architecture for American cities. Root's achievement on LaSalle Street certainly demonstrates the point Louis Sullivan later made, that in good architecture, "form ever follows function." The Rookery remains one of Chicago's best-loved buildings because in it Root showed how architecture that was deeply functional could be ornately beautiful as well.

John Wellborn Root

At the center of Chicago's architectural renaissance was John Wellborn Root. Born in Lumpkin, Georgia, Root pursued his studies in England, partly to avoid the Civil War. In England, he was struck by many architectural splendors, particularly the Gothic cathedrals. Returning to the United States, he worked in New York with the firm that designed and built the train shed at the first Grand Central Station in 1871 (since replaced). That iron-and-glass marvel, the nation's largest enclosure at the time, also inspired Root, and at a young age he discerned that good architecture was born of its age and environment. With an ambition to build great buildings, he imagined that his architecture might "convey in some large elemental sense an idea of the great, stable, conserving forces of modern civilization," as he later wrote in one of his many essays.

Root settled in Chicago by 1872 at the age of twenty-two, drawn like so many architects by the building boom that followed the Fire. In the intensity of the city at this time, Root felt a swirl of ideas that he might convey, ranging from the teeming forces of commerce requiring new office blocks to the revolutionary techniques in construction that were available for building them. Chicago's explosive growth—particularly that of its central business district, the Loop—made it the place to be for any ambitious young person at this time, especially a deep-thinking architect.

Root's talent was obvious when he presented himself for employment to Peter Wight, a leader among Chicago architects at the time. When the two met, Root showed Wight his drawings, and the older man was impressed. They were original, Wight later recalled, and Root appeared to grasp "the constructive principles of the best Gothic work of the twelfth and thirteenth centuries, to the materials, facilities, and necessities of our own time." In a period when truth in architecture was considered key, this was high praise.

Root's artistic side was matched by a high level of technical skill, and this gift in particular made it possible for him in 1873 to go off on his own and form a new firm with another young architect of the city, Daniel Burnham. While Burnham proved himself to be a bold visionary and grand promoter of the firm, christened Burnham & Root, Root won his reputation as a master designer. Few had a better understanding of foundations, metal frames, plate glass windows, and fireproofing, the building technologies that were making skyscrapers possible.

The Rookery was properly regarded as a skyscraper when it was built, but it never aspired to soar in the manner of the Board of Trade at the end of LaSalle Street. John Root was expressing in his design the solidity of this building, not dizzying height.

Photograph Jon Miller © Hedrich Blessing

It may have been Root's engineering intuition that brought new clients to the office, but once there they never failed to be impressed by his artistic side. Root regarded the complexities of commercial office buildings (the commissions of choice at the time) as fine artistic opportunities, so he worked out schemes for maximum space on the limited real estate of the Loop, designed foundations for the unstable soil, and created additional openings for more natural light. In effect, he thought of his buildings as works of art. In the architecture of office buildings, he wrote, "should be carried out the ideas of modern business life—simplicity, stability, breadth, and dignity." Root never flinched in his effort to express the splendors of commerce. Large office buildings should stand "refined, self-contained, sympathetic, discrete, urban, and modest," he wrote. It was a tall order, and still taller as skyscrapers rose to unprecedented heights.

An Epic Novel

One could say that John Wellborn Root's all-too-brief career in Chicago was a miracle of history, a story that touches numberless themes of modern architecture. Along with the strikingly simple Monadnock Building nearby, the elaborately decorative Rookery stands as Root's masterpiece. "It is an epic novel," says restoration architect T. Gunny Harboe, AIA, of McClier, who headed the effort to bring the Rookery to a pristine state in the early 1990s. Indeed, the building crystallizes so many ideas, and its story comprises so many willful characters, that the Rookery fairly reflects the drama of an early Chicago novel.

Richard Nickel, the great preservationist and photographer, saw the Rookery as he saw many buildings, when they were underappreciated by the rest of the world.

By the 1960s, the glass ceiling in the light court had been painted over to stop leaks. But Nickel still saw a lush interior—a mix of influences of Root, Wright, and, from 1931, William Drummond, whose contribution here is the protruding staircase from the balcony to the main floor (right-hand side above and bottom left on facing page).

Richard Nickel also documented the absolutely critical element of the large light well that made it possible to extend the almost square building to the extremities of the property on all four sides.

Much like the novels of the period, the Rookery's story begins with a wealthy financier, Peter Brooks. The Rookery's principal investor, Brooks was a Bostonian who rarely came to Chicago but had utter faith in the city's great and wealthy future. Brooks first became active in the Loop in 1879, acquiring an office block at Dearborn and Washington Streets through the fore-closure of a mortgage. Brooks had no aesthetic pretensions. Root viewed him as a developer "oblivious to matters of style" as far as architecture was concerned. Still, Brooks's role in skyscraper development is undeniable. In the period when builders went no higher than four or five stories, he wrote to an associate: "Tall buildings will pay well in Chicago, and sooner or later a way will be found to erect them."

In the speculative fury of these post-Fire years, Brooks and his investors bought more property in the Loop and planned new buildings. Brooks intelligently chose Burnham & Root to design them, learning of them through Brooks's Chicago-based partner, Owen Aldis. Legend has it that Aldis met Root at a reception and was impressed by the architect's ideas about architecture. Root believed that "practical conditions" governed design, as the architect later wrote, and that "underlying structure must dictate absolutely the general departure of external forms."

During construction in 1886 and 1887, the Rookery required a high level of personal craftsman-ship that marked the golden age of Chicago architecture. A major influence on Root and many contemporary American architects was Richardsonian Romanesque, exemplified in the Rookery by the entry arches on Adams Street (above) and LaSalle Street (opposite page, marked "100")

Among details on the exterior were two pairs of these crows, or rooks, seemingly laughing at the joke that a distinguished Chicago office block should be named for the former city hall at the same site, known as a rookery after its noisome birds and corrupt aldermen.

Practicality was Brooks's byword, too. Thus began a long and useful collaboration, beginning in 1882 with the Montauk Block on Monroe Street. Daniel Burnham remembered the Montauk as the first building to be called a skyscraper, even though it was built of load-bearing brick walls and not a metal frame—the latter came to define so-called skyscraper construction. The Montauk rose to the unprecedented height of ten stories and was so notably plain and bereft of ornament that some passersby thought there was some mistake.

But Brooks was happy with the result and commissioned more buildings by Burnham & Root. These and other office buildings by other talented architects in Chicago in the 1880s marked the first surge of Chicago's commercial architectural style. This style, which became known as the Chicago School, assumed no doctrine. Its only "rule" was an absence of ornamental features copied from architecture of the past. Indeed, Brooks became known for discouraging any decoration at all. "The building throughout is to be for use and not for ornament," he wrote. "Its beauty will be in its all-adaptation to its use."

Brooks's preference for plain buildings guided Root in many designs. They set aside the dictum for unadorned architecture when they built the Rookery, however. Perhaps Brooks reasoned that prestige clients preferred something

In John Root's original design, wrought iron was a keynote of the interior. Traditional in form, these ornate elements were functional and provided the light court with a ceiling of strength and a light and airy effect.

more decorative, and when the Rookery was completed in 1888, it was impressively ornate, though ornate in a way that hardly anyone had seen before.

While Brooks reversed his partiality for plain buildings in the Rookery, he also reversed his predilection for pretentious names. From the beginning he had intended a noble-sounding Indian name. But it was not to be; the story of the Rookery's naming is another amusing though significant story relating to its creation. "Rookery" was the nickname for Chicago's old City Hall, which previously had been on this site. It was not much of a building, good mostly for crows, or rooks, that took up residence in its walls, and also for less-than-sterling politicians who populated the interior. Rookery, therefore, had a double meaning that Chicagoans enjoyed, and it was a name, the developers thought, worth keeping. It was another wise choice.

In subtle ways, the Rookery's ironic name and lush ornament made it unlike most other buildings in Chicago at the time. But in retrospect the Rookery's idiosyncrasies show that the principles of the Chicago School were as flexible and open to change as were Root, the ambitious artist, and Burnham, the discerning entrepreneur.

One of Chicago's most beloved architectural features is the Rookery's "oriel" staircase. Root created a mesmerizing spiral that reflected the strength of iron and the lavish freedom of such a grand space, but most of all the fertile architectural imagination of Root himself.

Photograph by Nick Merrick of Hedrich Blessing, courtesy McClier

The 1992 restoration brought the oriel staircase back to its original glory. City code had changed in the meantime, however, and a new handrail had to be added above the old one.

Photograph by Nick Merrick of Hedrich Blessing, courtesy McClier

In the dramatic light well, an iron frame supported walls that could be opened with windows of maximum size. Some historians regard these as the first "ribbon windows," continuous bands of glass that became part of the modernist vocabulary a half-century later. The bulge in the wall at left is the exterior of the oriel staircase. The skylight at the top was added in the 1992 restoration.

Root's exterior was a worthy experiment in the design of a tall building. While unity is missing in some aspects of the exterior, the tireless patterns and overall design reflect the effort of an architect determined to discover a new architecture for the grandeur of the American spirit.

Photograph by Nick Merrick of Hedrich Blessing, courtesy McClier

As American architects of the late 1800s were struggling to free themselves from classical European architecture, they frequently used the massive arch, Romanesque in form but inspired by American strength and solidity, and a frequent element of commercial buildings of the period.

The Rookery's Practical Splendor

Root designed the Rookery from the inside out, around the building's luxurious light court and atrium. This space, one of the most fascinating and delightful ever constructed in Chicago, is built from the bottom of a broad light well that runs through the center of the almost square building. More than two stories above-ground are an expansive glass ceiling and decorative iron supports. Around the perimeter, an entresol balcony and elaborate cast-iron railing ring the

Photograph by Nick Merrick of Hedrich Blessing, courtesy McClier

Courtesy Chicago Architecture Foundation Archive

Shortly after Root's building was completed, it provoked ample discussion, most of it positive, about the Moorish designs that were regarded as so curious.

atrium. Root's dramatic stairways fill vertical space, and signs of loftiness are everywhere, including the "oriel" staircase, opening along the side of the light court and winding vertiginously upward.

The Rookery immediately impressed the critics. "There is nothing bolder, more original or more inspiring in modern civic architecture," wrote the Eastern critic Henry Van Brunt, "than its glass-covered court." This was high praise from the East, to which Chicago often looked for affirmation. But what impressed critics and practicing architects even more was the interplay between the visible and invisible elements of the building. These included Root's "floating" foundation, essentially an iron-reinforced slab across the entire foundation, that overcame the difficulty of Chicago's soggy soil.

The Rookery also became noted for the hybrid nature of its construction— part masonry and part metal frame. Iron and steel were in the process of changing architecture forever. A few years before the Rookery, Chicago architect William Le Baron Jenney completed the Home Insurance Building in 1885. It was framed almost entirely in iron, and the skeleton was covered in brick— making it what some have regarded as the first true skyscraper. The Rookery's owners, perhaps leery of a wholly metal frame, asked for masonry walls on the exterior. Root complied but used cast and wrought iron for interior supports and for the wall around the light court.

This iron frame was useful for a number of reasons. It was quicker and easier to assemble. It was also lighter in weight and placed less stress on the foundation. Most importantly, perhaps, it enabled Root to cover the walls of the light well inside with large sheets of glass. To Root, large windows as well

The Rookery's lighting fixtures are among several features of the interior light court, renovated in 1907 by Frank Lloyd Wright. Many aspects of this renovation are classic Wright, but none compromises the primary strength of John Root's original design.

as the atrium's glass ceiling were key. "The first radical question to suggest itself is that of light," he once wrote about planning any commercial structure. Here, Root did more than answer the practical question; in his inimitable way, his functional features were inextricably connected to the Rookery's staggering artistry. Even today, the restored Rookery attracts high-end tenants, not only with bright, airy office space but also with an aesthetic experience in the iron-and-glass atrium that continues to dazzle.

An Eclectic Exterior

The exterior of the Rookery appears less than modern to current eyes, and even in the early days, its heavy facade suffered its critics. Montgomery Schuyler of New York, one of the first to write of Chicago's leadership in American architecture, voiced his doubts, marveling at the Rookery's interior but calling its exterior "not architecturally so successful." Others complained that the elevations were too ornamental, as developer Brooks did when he saw the initial drawings. Even Root wrote in his journal that "I'm still ambivalent about the use of ornament, because decoration should never be applied to conceal the outline and intent of the more elementary and essential features of the building."

Still, the Rookery's arches, turrets, and traceries represent a bold step forward in skyscraper architecture of the time. Clearly, the exterior was inspired by what was called Richardsonian Romanesque, a style that was becoming important at this time among architects in search of a new "American" architecture. H. H. Richardson's version of Romanesque, of which the now-demolished

Photograph by Nick Merrick of Hedrich Blessing, courtesy McClier

In 1905, building management deemed a modernization desirable and hired the brilliant young architect who then had an office in the Rookery, Frank Lloyd Wright. Wright's main contribution was covering the dark iron surfaces of the old with panels of incised Carrara marble. In the 1992 restoration, a portion of Wright's marble in the near column was removed to reveal Root's original ironwork underneath. It was also here that the protruding staircase added by William Drummond in 1931 (see pages 20 and 21) was removed.

The lighting fixtures of Wright's renovation are similar to those Wright created for Unity Temple, one of the architect's most mold-breaking interiors. His Rookery renovation was completed around the same time, which leads to questions of Root's influence on Wright's conception of infinitely complex and alluring space. Prior to the 1992 restoration (probably sometime in the 1960s), the fixtures were inexplicably painted white (facing page).

In Wright's Adams Street lobby, the incised pattern is based on the "Arabian" designs in Root's original ornament and on designs from *The Grammar of Ornament* by Owen Jones. As this required complete reconstruction in the 1992 restoration, new blocks of Carrara marble were selected near the original source in Tuscany to match the tone and veining of that which Wright used almost ninety years earlier.

Photograph © Hedrich Blessing

Wright's changes to the Root design included most of the decorative railing panels in the stairs and balcony, but not here. These copper-plated cast-iron panels near the LaSalle Street entrance are Root's original design.

Marshall Field Wholesale Store of 1887 on Adams Street was a prime example, was considered "structurally expressive" and a true reflection of American simplicity and power.

While Richardsonian architecture was already influential, neither this nor any other style had been successfully applied to the design of tall buildings. Previous skyscrapers of ten stories or so resembled a number of low-lying buildings stacked one on top of the other— "like so many layers of cake," as the later critic William Jordy once wrote. Root was striving to overcome this issue—to express constructive principles as well as spiritual character in the tall office building.

The architect's attempt in the Rookery may have met with mixed success, but it was entirely original in its execution. Solid Romanesque entry arches are part of its heavily rusticated base, along with broad openings for windows. Moorish, Byzantine, and Venetian motifs—many with long vertical elements— draw the eye skyward. It cannot be said that the Rookery's specific exterior style was influential in its own day or any time later. But it was indeed an original style. It also demonstrated the power of "Root's fervid and fanciful pencil," remarked an admirer at the time.

Renovations

While much of the Loop's nineteenth-century architecture has been lost to demolition, the Rookery has survived intact as a rental building, as useful today as it was when it was built. Its longevity has been aided by three major renovations since the building's beginning, each bringing something new but each suggestive of the Rookery's original power.

Photograph by Nick Merrick of Hedrich Blessing, courtesy McClier

In the LaSalle Street entrance, the Wright-designed pattern in this broad panel was based on ornamental motifs in the marble arch (partially visible above) designed by Root for the original entrance. This entire section was lost in a later renovation, however, and re-created by the restoration architects of McClier.

In his remodeling of 1907, Frank Lloyd Wright replaced Root's elevator grills with his own design (facing page). One excellent aspect of the 1931 restoration by Wright's protégé William Drummond was the Art Deco–style elevators (above).

When architects surveyed the Rookery in the early 1990s, its atrium ceiling (seen here from above) was blackened over. After the 1992 restoration by Baldwin Development and McClier, the glass-and-iron structure was made pristine (facing page), and the Rookery became what Root had intended from the beginning. "The first radical question to suggest itself is that of light," he wrote with regard to the design of commercial buildings.

The first renovation, in 1905–1907, was inspired more by changing tastes than by any need to upgrade the building, which already was enjoying prestigious tenants, including architect Frank Lloyd Wright, whose Prairie School style was becoming fashionable. Perhaps Wright's presence in the building alerted the owners that a more modern profile might maintain the Rookery's status as one of the Loop's finest rental buildings. In any case, Wright under-

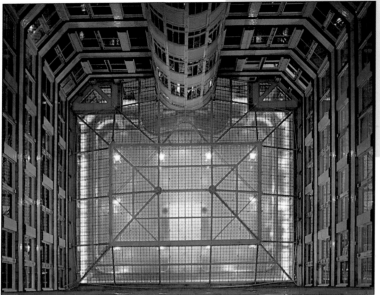

took the renovation, replacing some of Root's stunning fin-de-siècle detail while leaving other aspects of the light court intact.

In fact, Wright exercised notable restraint in the Rookery, at least by the standards of his imperious ego, suggesting what we already know: that Wright, like Root, was obsessed with the creation of a new architecture to express the American character. Wright's approach emphasized the importance of interior space, "the architecture of the within," as he described it in his writing.

When he received the Rookery commission, Wright was also in the throes of designing his early triumphs—the Larkin Building in Buffalo, New York, and Unity Temple in Oak Park, Illinois. In his writings, Wright described these projects in terms of his effort to "break the box" of traditional architecture and create buildings with "freedom of space." Indeed, Root's atrium clearly expresses much of what Wright himself sought— architecture that could defeat the sense of enclosure.

Between 1905 and 1907, Wright simplified but did not radically alter the Root design, primarily through the use of incised marble and gold leaf. Wright's renovation represents a departure from the original, but Wright's respect for Root is evident everywhere, particularly as he carved designs in the marble that echo Root's original patterns in wrought iron. Wright's renovation seems sympathetic to Root's intention. Today, white marble and gold leaf highlights create luminescent effects that Root himself would have appreciated.

In 1931, architect William Drummond was given the commission for a new renovation of the Rookery's public spaces. Here major work, including sleek new Art Deco designs, indicated that the Rookery still played a positive role in Chicago's commercial center. Less positive was the architectural message— the once-lofty entranceways at the LaSalle and Adams Street doors were cut down to size with a floor overhead, sacrificing the openness of the lobbies but creating additional rentable space. Enclosing space that was once open was a major legacy of the Drummond renovation, although graceful incising on bronze elevator doors—naturalistic representations of birds and flora— reveal ties to the light and airy spirit of the Rookery going back to Root.

Photograph Jon Miller © Hedrich Blessing

LaSalle Street has changed over the years. The Bank of America building in the foreground was built in 1923. The Harris Bank Building in the background is postwar modern. But the timeless character of LaSalle Street resides in the inimitable Rookery.

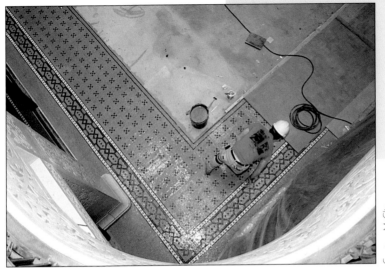

Re-creating mosaic floor pavement required extrapolating from the fragments that remained. Marble tesserae were assembled at a latter-day mosaic shop, laid at the site, and smoothed with a terrazzo grinder for the uniform surface achieved in the original, although with considerably less effort than had been involved a century before.

Courtesy McClier

In 1992, the most recent and most extensive renovation of the Rookery demonstrated that the building could be returned to first-class office space, despite its age and despite the toll that time and neglect had taken on many buildings of its era. Clearly, this renovation required the recovery of architectural values that had been diminished if not lost. But by the late 1980s, the developer Baldwin Development Company began the project with resolve

During the McClier restoration, it was discovered that John Root's wrought iron columns were still hidden inside Wright's marble ones. In one case, restoration architect T. Gunny Harboe, AIA, decided to leave one side of a marble column open (top left photograph) to illustrate the work of both architects. Also in this area is the section of original mosaic floor (above). Together these elements comprise the Rookery's "interpretive corner," where stories of the building can be seen in layers.

In this lovely section of carved marble, restoration architects McClier saw to it that the carving was finished with chisels to preserve the handmade effect. Gold leaf was applied much as it was during the days of Root and Wright. As in the past, the sun streaming through the atrium ceiling makes this rich and elaborate work living and ever changing.

To restore much of the marble that was lost in the 1931 renovation, old photographs were projected and enlarged, and pattern books were consulted, particularly the one authored by Owen Jones, *The Grammar of Ornament*, which both Root and Wright used. Full-size plans were created and set in their proper place, and the panels were finished by hand.

Courtesy McClier

Members of the restoration team traveled to Carrara, Italy, to find pieces of marble to match those left from the Wright renovation. The job required four large blocks to be hewn from the quarry and cut to the requisite shapes and sizes in Italy. The resulting panels were shipped to the United States and then carved and installed.

to marry the importance of the Rookery's LaSalle Street location with the building's timeless sense of architecture.

Renewing the Rookery's splendor was not a simple matter. It required significant private wealth to overcome corporate resistance to expense without certain return. L. Thomas Baldwin III was a successful futures trader with the luxury to create a commercial building in a museumlike environment. With the assistance of McClier as restoration architects, Baldwin's challenge was to invest in a historic structure and simultaneously meet the needs of high-end commercial tenants.

For restoration architect Harboe, who oversaw the project for McClier, the objective was to create a near-pristine result at a sustainable cost. To achieve the goal, they used highly advanced techniques, including computer technology, to complete full sections of mosaic floor and other ornament. Yet other techniques were as hands-on, in some cases, as the original. In carving new marble panels—from Carrara, which was the source of the originals—the intricate tracery was begun by machine but finished with hand chisels, thus replicating the tactile effect of the old incisions.

Other aspects of this restoration project were more invisible, such as the decision of whose designs to restore, Root's or Wright's? Or a combination to include the designs of Drummond? In fact, the hybrid approach was selected based partially on the stature of Root and Wright in particular, and partly on the ability to restore what was in fact there. While the original Root design appears in photographs as a fascinating space from a vibrant and charming period, Harboe explains that returning the atrium to its pre-Wright design would have required too much conjecture.

In the end, the restoration of the Rookery was another stroke of good fortune for a building that has enjoyed good fortune for more than a century. Certainly it was blessed by the recent maturity within the practice of restoration architecture. From the initial vision for the Rookery restoration to the small details that create the symphonies that architects sometimes call buildings, the Baldwin-McClier project unfolded with the intelligence and (sometimes) an expense-be-damned decisiveness that one might associate with . . . well, Frank Lloyd Wright.

By 1992, when the restoration was complete, the "new" Rookery opened to praise from the architectural community and a new surge of affection from the public. It debuted as an apparition from the past, a sparkling stage set from a golden moment in history. It was more than that, however. The Rookery demonstrated that large buildings that make an impact represent more than one point in time and the spirit of just one single architect. They represent various moments in time and the sometimes-rich "conversation," in architectural parlance, among architect, client, successive architects, and ultimately, several generations of public taste.

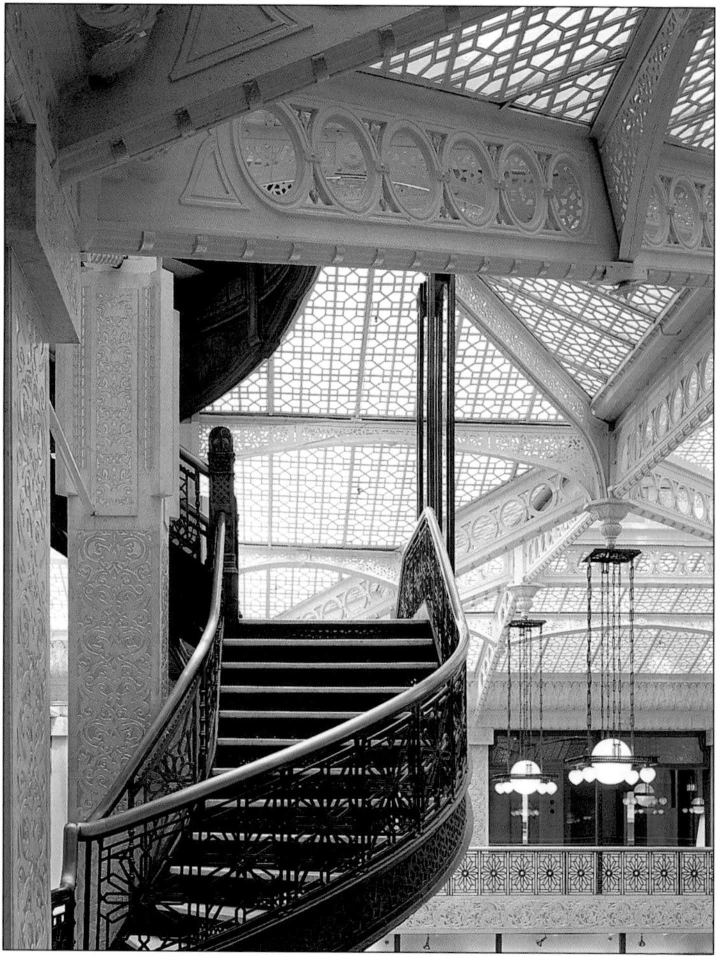

The Rookery, now a first-class office building owned by Rookery L.L.C., provides endless fascination in the way the interior penetrates exterior space, the luminescence of light on gold leaf, and sensations that defy gravity. As striking as the ironwork, glass, pavements, and other elements of this building appear, it is the intangible elements such as the movement of space and the play of light that make the Rookery a favorite among visitors to Chicago architectural landmarks. Since it was built, the Rookery has remained a towering influence on American architecture.

Even though surrounded by newer and taller buildings, the Rookery remains today an imposing presence on LaSalle Street in the midst of the Loop's financial district. The Rookery is also one of the most beloved buildings in Chicago.